RIVER ADVENTURES
YANGTZE RIVER

A+

Smart Apple Media

Published by Smart Apple Media
P.O. Box 3263, Mankato, Minnesota 56002
www.smartapplemedia.com

U.S. publication copyright © 2016 Smart Apple Media.
International copyright reserved in all countries. No
part of this book may be reproduced in any form
without written permission from the publisher.

Published by arrangement with the Watts Publishing
Group LTD, London.

Library of Congress Cataloging-in-Publication Data

Manning, Paul, 1954-
 The Yangtze River / Paul Manning.
    p. cm. -- (River adventures)
 Summary: "Beginning on a plateau in Tibet, readers
will journey down Asia's longest river in this exciting
adventure. Traveling through China, readers will learn
about the rare Yangtze dolphins, terraced farmlands,
various cultures, the giant Three Gorges Dam, and
much more!"--Provided by publisher.
 Includes index.
 ISBN 978-1-59920-919-7 (library binding)
 1. Yangtze River (China)--Juvenile literature. I. Title.
 DS793.Y3M36 2015
 919.512--dc23

                              2012035420

ISBN: 978-1-59920-919-7   (library binding)
ISBN: 978-1-62588-589-0   (eBook)

Designed, edited, and produced by Paul Manning
Maps by Stefan Chabluk

Printed in the United States by CG Book Printers
North Mankato, Minnesota

PO 1732
3-2015

9 8 7 6 5 4 3 2 1

Note to Teachers and Parents

Every effort has been made to ensure that the Websites
listed on page 32 are suitable for children, that they are
of the highest educational value and that they contain
no inappropriate or offensive material. However,
because of the nature of the Internet, it is impossible
to guarantee that the content of these sites will not be
altered. We strongly recommend that Internet access is
supervised by a responsible adult.

Key to Images

Top cover image: Pudong district, Shanghai
Main cover image: Cormorant fishing on the Yangtze
Previous page: Cormorant with alligator gar fish
This page: The Three Gorges Dam, Hubei province,
China.

Picture Credits

CONTENTS

A Yangtze Journey

The Yangtze is Asia's longest river, stretching for 3,915 miles (6,300 km). Its Chinese name is Chang Jiang, which means the "Long River." You will follow the river from its **source** on the Qinghai–Tibet Plateau to where it drains into the East China Sea near Shanghai.

A Great River

Chinese civilization began on the banks of the Yangtze. For thousands of years, Chinese people have relied on the river for transport, **irrigating** crops, and for food and water. Today, about half of all the food in China is grown in the Yangtze **basin**, including more than two-thirds of the country's rice crop. Almost 500 million people live and work along its banks.

▼ The Yangtze flows through many different landscapes, including farmed hillsides, mountains, forests, **fertile** plains, and wetlands.

Threats to the Yangtze

In recent years, the river has become polluted by factory and household waste. Wildlife **habitats** have been destroyed, and many types of fish that once lived in the river have disappeared. The Chinese government is working to repair the damage and to protect endangered species. Some sections of the river have now been made into nature reserves.

The Yangtze's Source

Finding the source of a river like the Yangtze is not easy because many other streams, called **tributaries***, flow into it. People once thought that the Jinsha Jiang River was the source. Then, in 1976, a small lake was discovered at the foot of Mount Geladandong near the border with Tibet. Most now agree that this lake is the Yangtze's source.*

MONGOLIA

ASIA

AFRICA

Key

☐ Neighbouring countries
☐ Provinces adjoining the Yangtze River

CHINA

Mount Geladandong

QINGHAI–TIBET PLATEAU

SICHUAN PROVINCE

Tiger Leaping Gorge

INDIA

Shigu   Lijiang

YUNNAN PROVINCE

MYANMAR (BURMA)

VIETNAM

Jinsha Jiang River

Yangtze River

Chongqing
Fengdu

Qutang Gorge

Wu Gorge

Xiling Gorge

Gezhouba Dam

Three Gorges dam and reservoir

Fengjie

HUBEI PROVINCE

Hou River

Sandouping

Yichang

Sashi

JANGXI PROVINCE

Beijing

Grand Canal

Yellow Sea

JIANGSU PROVINCE

ANHUI PROVINCE

Zhenjiang   Huangpu River

Nanjing

Lake Taihu

Shanghai

Wuhan

Hangzhou

Hukou

South China Sea

▼ Because of pollution and other threats, scientists fear that the Yangtze dolphin may have died out completely.

YOU ARE HERE

Map labels: CHINA, Mt. Geladandong, Qinghai–Tibet Plateau, SICHUAN, Yangtze River, Shigu, YUNNAN

The Tibetan Plateau

The Yangtze's source, Mount Geladandong, is high on the Qinghai–Tibet Plateau in western China. As you fly over the plateau, you can see how vast and remote this region is.

▼ The Tibetan Plateau is sometimes called the "roof of the world." It is four times the size of France. Many of the great rivers of Asia begin here.

The Upper Yangtze

The Yangtze begins by flowing east through a shallow valley. It then winds south past snow-covered mountain peaks that are cut with steep rocky valleys called **gorges**. On flat parts of the plateau, tribesmen live by herding cattle. These **nomads** do not have a permanent home, but move from place to place, living in circular tents called **yurts**.

▼ The first turn of the Yangtze is at Shigu in Yunnan Province where the river heads northeast.

The Yangtze's First Turn

For several hundred miles, the Yangtze flows southeast. At a small town called Shigu, it meets a massive wall of limestone and suddenly turns northeast. This is known as the "first turn" of the Yangtze.

Until 50 years ago, this part of China was cut off from the rest of the world. Its people lived under their own rulers. Today, roads and railways are being built, and the way of life is changing. But many areas are still very remote. Some villages are so isolated that they can be reached only by mountain paths and rope bridges.

The Kazak People

*The mountains of northwestern China are home to approximately 800,000 nomadic Kazak people. In the summer, they set up their homes in the high mountains, where there are **pastures** for their cattle. When autumn comes, they move lower down, packing up their tents and taking their belongings with them.*

▶ A Kazak family leaves the plains in search of fresh pastures.

SICHUAN

Yangtze River

Tiger Leaping Gorge

Lijiang

YUNNAN

YOU ARE HERE

Tiger Leaping Gorge

At Lijiang, approximately 12 miles (20 km) east of Shigu, you catch a bus to Tiger Leaping Gorge. Over millions of years, this dramatic gorge has been carved out of the rock by the fast-flowing Yangtze River.

▼ Tiger Leaping Gorge is one of the world's deepest gorges. Its name comes from a local legend in which a tiger escaped from a hunter by leaping across the river.

At Tiger Leaping Gorge, the Yangtze falls 985 feet (300 m) over a series of 18 **rapids**. Below the viewing point where you are standing now, the river hurtles through a gap just 100 feet (30 m) wide. The roar of the water echoes off sheer rock walls, which tower up to 9,850 feet (3,000 m) high on either side of you.

▲ The ancient city of Lijiang was once an important trading and cultural center. Today, its income comes mainly from tourism.

The Naxi

Returning to Lijiang, you explore the old part of the city with its narrow, cobbled streets and traditional wooden houses.

The people of this area, called the Naxi, have a rich history. Originally from Tibet, they settled here more than a thousand years ago. In the past, the Naxi lived by farming and herding. Since tourists started visiting Lijiang, many Naxi people now earn a living by making goods to sell in local shops.

The Lijiang Earthquake

In 1996, a major earthquake struck the Lijiang region. About a third of the city was destroyed, including many of its oldest buildings. Afterward, Lijiang was rebuilt and developed as a center for tourism. Many people now visit the region and learn about the culture of the Naxi people.

▶ Naxi people follow an ancient religion called Dongba. They worship the natural world around them, including the sun, moon, mountains, and rivers.

Farming the Valleys

In the mountains around Lijiang, farmers have cut steps into the hillsides to create level strips of land called terraces. These are used for growing crops.

YOU ARE HERE

▼ On steep hillside plots, plowing with buffalo or oxen is easier than using a tractor.

Terracing

Stone walls help to support the terraces and hold the soil in place. The farmers also cut ditches to carry water from nearby streams to their fields. Much of the farm work is done by hand, but water buffalo are used to plow the fields before planting.

Erosion

In the Upper Yangtze, the heavy storms of the rainy season occur in spring and summer. When it rains, water pours down the slopes, washing away crops and soil. This causes the land to erode.

When too many trees are cut down or animals are allowed to overgraze the land, **erosion** can be a big problem. Since the 1950s, many forests along the Yangtze have been cut down for timber or firewood. Without the trees to hold the land together, soil is washed into the river. This makes the channel shallow and muddy and increases the danger of flooding.

▲ Trees and terraced strips help to protect this fertile soil around Lijiang from being washed away by heavy rains.

Deforestation

Land in the Yangtze basin has been damaged by **deforestation**. After disastrous floods in 1998, the Chinese government decided it was time to act. Laws were passed to prevent the cutting of trees and overgrazing. Local people were made aware of the dangers of cutting down trees, and new trees were planted in deforested areas.

Chongqing

SICHUAN

Chongqing

Yangtze River

Lijiang

YUNNAN

YOU ARE HERE

At Chongqing, you reach the first big city on your journey. This great trading and industrial center began as a riverside port. It is now one of the biggest cities in China and one of the fastest-growing cities in the world.

▼ Industrial fumes pollute the air over Chongqing, the biggest inland river port in western China.

The Yangtze has been vital to the growth of Chongqing. From the city's docks, millions of tons of cargo are transported along the river every day. Since the building of the Three Gorges Dam, big ships can now travel here all the way from the East China Sea.

▶ Factories in Chongqing produce everything from textiles to electrical goods. Nearly all the goods produced here are transported out of the city by river.

Industrial Growth

The old city of Chongqing dates back to the fourth century. Built on the clifftops and flanked by the river to the west, it was a natural fortress and easy to defend.

In the 1970s, the Chinese government chose Chongqing as a center of industrial growth, and many new factories were built here. Since then, it has expanded at an amazing rate. Around 30 million people now live in the Chongqing region, and half a million more arrive every year.

A Veil of Fog

During the spring and autumn, a thick layer of fog covers Chongqing. In recent years, smoke and pollution from factories have made the problem worse, and a haze of fumes called **smog** hangs in the air. The poor air quality is bad for people's health. The city's government is now trying to reduce the pollution.

The Flooded Valley

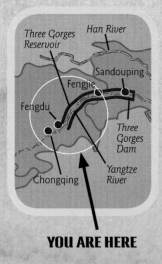

Three Gorges
Reservoir
Han River
Sandouping
Fengjie
Fengdu
Three
Gorges
Dam
Chongqing
Yangtze
River

YOU ARE HERE

At Chongqing, you board a passenger boat for the next leg of your journey. This part of the river has been transformed by the building of the Three Gorges Dam downstream.

Drowned Cities

▼ Since the flooding of the river valley, the Yangtze carries more traffic than ever. This carrier is transporting a cargo of trucks from a factory in Chongqing.

When the dam was built, the entire river valley between Chongqing and Sandouping was flooded. This now forms a **reservoir** 398 miles (640 km) long. Thirteen cities were rebuilt higher up the river banks, and thousands of acres of farmland disappeared underwater. The flooding of the valley has changed this part of China forever.

◀ This new town was built to re-house people who lost their homes due to the building of the Three Gorges Dam.

More than a million people were ordered to leave their homes to make way for the dam. Although they were given money by the government, many did not want to leave the homes where they had lived for generations.

River Traffic

Since the valley was flooded, the river has risen by as much as 570 feet (175 m). This has opened the way for many more ships to use the river. In the past, sand and gravel on the riverbed were a danger to shipping. Oceangoing ships now can travel the river safely. This extra traffic has brought great wealth to Chongqing and other cities farther downriver.

The "Ghost City" of Fengdu

*Dating back 1,800 years, the "Ghost City" of Fengdu was an ancient burial site that was famous for its statues of demons and devils. Since the flooding of the river valley, much of the city is now underwater and most of the original **shrines** have been lost.*

YOU ARE HERE

The Three Gorges

At Fengjie, you board a cruise boat to explore the Three Gorges. These spectacular limestone gorges stretch for 80 miles (130 km). They are among the most famous sights in China.

▼ River cruises on the Yangtze are a growing source of income for the Three Gorges region.

Qutang Gorge, the first of the three gorges, is the shortest and narrowest. The mountains on either side are 3,900 feet (1,200 m) high and tower over the river. Along the sides of the gorge, you can still see ancient pathways carved into the rock where teams of men once hauled boats upstream.

◀ The point where the river passes between these mountains is called the Kuimen Gate. It marks the entrance to Qutang Gorge.

The Yangtze Gorges

Experts believe that the Yangtze River first began to cut a path through the mountains 45 million years ago. The transport route formed by the river has been vital to China ever since. Without it, the fertile Sichuan Province, "China's rice bowl," would have been almost completely cut off from the rest of the country.

In Wu Gorge, an ancient legend tells how 12 wild dragons brought chaos and floods to the land. They were defeated by Yao Ji, daughter of the Queen Mother of the West. After her death, Yao Ji and her sisters were turned into 12 great mountain peaks—six on either side of the gorge.

The third gorge, Xiling, is 47 miles (76 km) long. In the past, travelers often drowned in the powerful **whirlpools** and rapids here. Since the river valley was flooded, Xiling has become less dangerous, but boats still keep between markers that show the safest route.

▶ People have traveled the Yangtze in boats since ancient times. This traditional type of sailing boat is called a "junk."

Three Gorges Dam

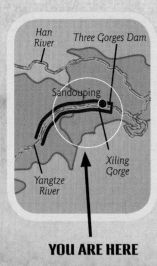

YOU ARE HERE

As you leave Xiling Gorge, you come face to face with one of the great wonders of modern China—the huge Three Gorges Dam.

▼ As well as reducing the risk of flooding, the giant Three Gorges Dam supplies 10 percent of China's energy needs.

An Engineering Triumph

The dam is a great achievement for China. For centuries, floods along the Yangtze brought suffering to the Chinese people. The dam controls the flow of the river and reduces the risk of flooding. It is also the world's largest **hydroelectric** plant, producing vital energy for China's fast-growing towns and cities.

◀ This huge **lock** allows ships and cargo boats to bypass the Three Gorges Dam and continue on their journey along the river.

The Impact of the Dam

Since it was completed in 2009, the Three Gorges Dam has brought prosperity to many parts of China, but not all its effects have been good.

As well as forcing people to leave their homes, it has harmed wildlife and the environment. Rubbish and pollution have built up in the dam reservoir, and fish have been poisoned. Water from the dam reservoir has eroded the hillsides, and many parts of the river valley have been affected by landslides. Some experts believe that the weight of water in the reservoir may even damage Earth's crust.

The Yangtze Floods

In the last century, thousands died as a result of flooding on the Yangtze. In 1998, the floods were among the worst ever, destroying homes, devastating crops and livestock, and leaving thousands dead or homeless. Despite the building of the Three Gorges Dam, flooding caused by heavy **monsoon** rains still affects many areas of the country.

▶ People rescue belongings during floods on the Yangtze in 2010.

Yichang to Wuhan

At Yichang, you leave the mountains and gorges behind. The river flows more slowly here, broadening out across flat, low-lying land. This is the start of the Yangtze's great **floodplain**.

Industrial Cities

As well as farming, there is industry on this part of the river. Electricity from the nearby Gezhouba Dam has turned Yichang into a fast-growing industrial city. About 93 miles (150 km) downstream, Shashi is another booming industrial town with cotton mills, **dyeworks**, and machinery plants.

▼ A cargo boat brings supplies of building materials to the city of Yichang.

◀ The 1957 Wuhan Yangtze Bridge was the first ever built across the Yangtze.

China Tea

In the nineteenth century, Hankou was a center of the tea trade. Ships from Great Britain sailed up the river to collect their cargo and raced for home. Tea spoils if it is kept too long at sea, so the fastest ships fetched the best prices. On one voyage, the famous Cutty Sark covered a record 362 nautical miles (670 km) in a single day.

Wuhan

The most important city in this region is Wuhan. Here, the Yangtze is joined by its longest tributary, the Han River.

Wuhan's main industry is iron, and steelmaking. The city dates back nearly 2,000 years. Three cities—Hankou, Hanyang, and Wuchang—grew up around the meeting of the rivers before eventually merging into one. It was not until 1957 that the cities were linked by a bridge across the Yangtze.

▶ Wuhan's Yellow Crane Tower is a famous landmark overlooking the river.

21

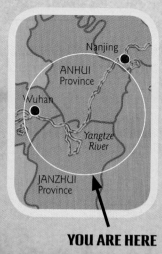

YOU ARE HERE

The Lower Yangtze

Beyond the city of Wuhan, you enter the "land of fish and rice." This fertile region produces around 70 percent of China's **paddy** rice and more than half of its freshwater fish.

Rice Growing

Rice is China's singlemost important food. Most of it is grown by the river in fields called "paddies." Rice plants need lots of water to grow. Some of the water comes from rain, but most is pumped from the river and piped to the nearby fields.

Once the rice has been picked, it is threshed to separate the waste from the grain and then stored. Finally, the field is plowed and made ready for a new crop to be planted.

▼ These flooded paddy fields need to be supplied with water all year round.

◀ Planting rice by hand is hard work in the hot sun.

Yangtze Silt

When the Yangtze floods, it brings with it a rich layer of **sediment** called **silt** that helps to nourish the soil and make it fertile. Since the building of the Three Gorges Dam, the river brings less silt because much of the sediment gets trapped in the huge reservoir behind the dam.

Fish from the River

The Yangtze has always been a rich source of fish, including carp, bream, perch, and sturgeon. With thousands of lakes around Wuhan, fishing and fish-farming are vital industries. Because of pollution and overfishing, the number of fish has declined recently. In some areas, fishing is now banned during the breeding season, so fish stocks have a chance to recover.

▶ This fisherman has birds called cormorants, which he has trained to help him catch fish in the river.

YOU ARE HERE

Nanjing

From Hukou, the Yangtze gently descends through plains, hills, lakes, and wetland before reaching the ancient city of Nanjing.

City Walls

As you enter the outskirts of Nanjing, the city's stone walls come into view. In earlier times, these high walls protected the people of the city from attack. Nowadays, the buildings of the old city are surrounded by high-rise blocks, modern shopping, and business districts.

▼ Old and new buildings line the river in the center of Nanjing.

24

▶ Nanjing's stone walls stretch for 20 miles (32 km) around the city.

Nanjing was once the capital of China and has often played an important part in the country's history. It is also a key commercial and industrial center, and many transport routes meet here.

The Grand Canal

About 50 miles (80 km) beyond Nanjing, you meet another important waterway. The Grand Canal runs between Beijing in the north and Hangzhou in the south, crossing the Yangtze at Zhenjiang. Stretching for 1,118 miles (1,800 km), the Grand Canal is the longest man-made waterway in the world.

▼ In places, the Grand Canal is so busy that extra channels have been built around major cities to reduce the traffic jams.

A Vital Waterway

The Grand Canal was completed nearly 2,000 years ago to allow farmers in southern China to transport grain to the northern cities. Nearly 6 million laborers helped to build it, and many died during its construction. Today, it is a vital route for barges carrying building materials to the rapidly developing delta area.

YOU ARE HERE

The Yangtze Delta

Below Nanjing, the Yangtze is tidal. This means that its flow is affected by the twice-daily rise and fall of the tides in the East China Sea.

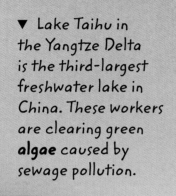

▼ Lake Taihu in the Yangtze Delta is the third-largest freshwater lake in China. These workers are clearing green **algae** caused by sewage pollution.

Draining the Delta

As the river approaches the sea, the incoming tide slows its movement. Silt is dropped to form a maze of marshy islands, sandbanks, and water channels. This is known as the river delta.

A hundred years ago, the Yangtze Delta was mostly swamp. Since then, many of the marshes have been drained and the river banks raised to protect against flooding. Today, the delta is one of the most crowded places on Earth with a population of more than 80 million.

◀ This new road bridge is part of a 15-mile (25-km) bridge and tunnel network connecting Shanghai with Chongming Island in the north.

Flood Protection

*There are about 1,050 miles (1,700 km) of flood barriers along the Yangtze. Many date back to ancient times. One of the oldest is the Zhenjiang **levee**. The 113-mile (182 km) dike protects 8 million people, two major cities, and 3,100 square miles (800,000 ha) of farmland.*

A Dynamic Region

As China's economy has grown, the Yangtze Delta has become heavily developed. To reduce overcrowding in the main city of Shanghai, more than a million people were moved to 10 new settlements in the delta. Each new town has its own industrial zone, mostly specializing in growth industries such as information and communications technology and electronics.

Meanwhile, in Shanghai, a huge plan was launched to rebuild the city's water supply system and reduce pollution. You will see the amazing growth of Shanghai as you reach the last stage of your journey.

▼ The Siberian Crane is among many migrating birds that winter in the Yangtze Delta.

YOU ARE HERE

Shanghai

At Shanghai, on the south side of the Yangtze Delta, you reach your journey's end. This busy city grew up as a trading center where the Huangpu River joins the Yangtze. Today, it has a key role in China's booming economy.

Pudong

Across the river from old Shanghai, Pudong is a powerful **symbol** of the new China. In 1990, it was little more than farmland. Today, it is a thriving business center covering more than 39 square miles (100 sq km). Many big companies have their headquarters in Pudong, and high-tech products manufactured here are exported all over the world.

▼ Shanghai's Pudong district is on the east bank of the Huangpu River. The Oriental Pearl Television Tower is the tallest building at 1,535 feet (468 m).

► Shanghai Port is the world's busiest container depot.

Puxi

Leaving your boat at Shanghai port, you stroll along the Bund, the main street of Puxi on the west bank of the Huangpu River.

Puxi is the historic center of Shanghai and home to nearly half the city's population. Along the riverfront, many of the old buildings were built by foreign traders. Today, luxury hotels and entertainment complexes are based here. The wide **embankment** is a popular place for local people and tourists to stroll.

A High-rise City

Shanghai's population of nearly 24 million makes it the largest city in China and the seventh largest in the world. With so many people to house and so little land to build on, the city's planners decided that the only way to build was up! In Shanghai, every skyscraper has to be built on deep concrete **piles** to keep it from sinking into the marshy ground of the delta.

▼ The famous street known as the Bund stretches for 1 mile (1.6 km) along the west bank of the Huangpu River.

Glossary

algae aquatic organisms that do not have roots, stems, or leaves

basin the area drained by a river

deforestation cutting down trees for timber or firewood

dyeworks factory where cloth is colored

embankment a high wall built to protect against flooding

erosion the wearing away of soil or rock

fertile good for growing crops

floodplain the area affected by a river's floodwaters

gorge a steep, rocky river valley

habitat the natural home of a plant or animal

hydroelectric electricity produced by water power

irrigating supplying water to a field to grow crops

levee a bank of earth that acts as a flood barrier

lock a way of altering the water level so that boats can bypass dams on a river

monsoon a seasonal wind that brings rain between June and August

nomad a person who moves from place to place

paddy a watery field where rice is grown

pasture grazing land for cattle

pile a slab of concrete that is driven into the ground to form the foundation for a building

rapids where water flows quickly over stones and boulders

reservoir a man-made lake for storing water

sediment stones and mud from the riverbed

shrine a place built as a memorial to someone who has died

silt fine sediment carried downstream by a river

smog a haze of fog and polluted air

source the place where a river begins

symbol something with special meaning

tributary a river or stream that flows into a larger one

whirlpool a dangerous stretch of water where the current circles downward

yurt a tent used by nomads in Tibet and Mongolia

Yangtze Quiz

Look up information in this book or online. Find the answers on page 32.

1 Match the captions to the pictures.

1

2

3

4

5

6

A A giant panda

B The City God Temple of Shanghai

C A Chinese lotus

D A Yangtze river cruiser

E A Tibetan yurt

F A Chinese man of the Naxi people

2 These places can all be found along the Yangtze. Place them in the right order, starting with the ones nearest to the sea:

Chongqing
Shigu
Wuhan
Shanghai
Lijiang
Fengjie

3 Where would you find the Meng Liang Staircase, the Ancient Plank Road, the Hanging Monk Rock, and the Seven Gate Cave?

4 What is this, and where would you find it?

Websites and Further Reading

Websites

- *www.kids.nationalgeographic.com/explore/countries/china*
  Good short introduction to China.

- *www.worldwildlife.org/places/yangtze*
  Useful information on Yangtze wildlife.

- *www.wwf.org.uk/where_we_work/asia/asian_rivers*
  Interesting material on environmental issues facing the Yangtze wetlands.

Further Reading

Aloian, Molly. *The Yangtze : China's Majestic River* (Rivers Around the world). Crabtree Pub. Co., 2010.

Rice, Earle Jr. *The Yangtze River* (Rivers of the World). Mitchell Lane Publishers, 2012.

Kite, Patricia. *Building the Three Gorges Dam.* Raintree, 2010.

Index

Answers to Yangtze Quiz
1 1B, 2C, 3A, 4F, 5D, 6E. **2** Shanghai, Wuhan, Fengjie, Chongqing, Lijiang, Shigu. **3** All four are man-made or natural features of Qutang Gorge, the longest of the Three Gorges. **4** One of the giant turbines of the Three Gorges Dam. Water from the dam drives the turbine, which generates hydroelectricity.